First World War

and Army of Occupation

War Diary

France, Belgium and Germany

16 DIVISION
47 Infantry Brigade
Black Watch (Royal Highlanders)
9th (Service) Battalion
1 May 1918 - 28 April 1919

WO95/1970/1

The Naval & Military Press Ltd
www.nmarchive.com
Published in association with The National Archives

Published by

The Naval & Military Press Ltd

Unit 10 Ridgewood Industrial Park,

Uckfield, East Sussex,

TN22 5QE England

Tel: +44 (0) 1825 749494

www.naval-military-press.com

www.nmarchive.com

This diary has been reprinted in facsimile from the original. Any imperfections are inevitably reproduced and the quality may fall short of modern type and cartographic standards.

Contents

Document type	Place/Title	Date From	Date To
Heading	WO95/1970 16 Div-47 Inf Bde 9 Black Watch May 1918-Apr 1919		
Heading	16th Division 47th Infy Bde 9th Black Watch (R.H.) May 1918-Apl 1919 From 15 Div 44 Bde		
Heading	War Diary of 9th Bn The Black Watch For May 1918 Volume V		
War Diary		01/05/1918	31/05/1918
Heading	9th (S) Btn. The Black Watch War Diary For June 1918 Volume VI		
Heading	9th (S) Bn. The Black Watch War Diary For August 1918 Volume. VII		
War Diary	In The Field	30/06/1918	31/08/1918
Heading	9th (S) Btn The Black Watch War Diary For September 1918 Volume VIII		
War Diary		01/09/1918	30/09/1918
Heading	9th (S) Btn. The Black Watch War Diary For October 1918 Volume IX		
War Diary		01/10/1918	31/10/1918
Operation(al) Order(s)	Operation Order No. 28		
Operation(al) Order(s)	9th Black Watch Order No.	24/10/1918	24/10/1918
Heading	9th (S) Btn. The Black Watch War Diary For November 1918 Volume X		
War Diary		01/11/1918	30/11/1918
Miscellaneous	Operation Order By Capt J.R. Philip H.Q. Commanding. App I	08/11/1918	08/11/1918
Miscellaneous	9th (S) Battn The Black Watch Operation Orders By Capt J.R.Philip R.S. Commanding. App II	10/11/1918	10/11/1918
Miscellaneous	9th (S) Battn The Black Watch Operation Order No. 28 App III	15/11/1918	15/11/1918
Miscellaneous	H.Q.		
Operation(al) Order(s)	9th Btn The Black Watch Order No 29 App IV	16/11/1918	16/11/1918
Miscellaneous	9th Btn The Black Watch Order No.30 App V	26/11/1918	26/11/1918
Heading	9th (S) Btn. The Black Watch War Diary For December 1918 Volume XI		
War Diary		01/12/1918	31/12/1918
Heading	9th (S) Btn. The Black Watch War Diary For January 1919 Volume XII		
War Diary		03/01/1919	31/01/1919
Heading	9th (S) Btn. The Black Watch War Diary For February 1919 Volume XIII		
War Diary		01/02/1919	28/02/1919
Heading	9th (S) Btn. The Black Watch War Diary For March 1919 Volume XIV		
War Diary	Trechen	01/03/1919	30/03/1919
Heading	9th (S) Btn. The Black Watch War Diary For April 1919 Volume XV		
War Diary	Pont A Marcq	02/04/1919	28/04/1919

WO95/1970

16 Div - 47 Inf Bde

9 Black Watch

May 1918 - Apr 1919

16TH DIVISION
47TH INFY BDE

BLACK WATCH (R.H.)
9TH ~~BN ROY. HDRS (B.W.)~~
MAY ~~JULY~~ 1918-APL 1919

From 15 Div 44 BDE

Instructions regarding War Diaries and Intelligence Summaries are contained in F. S. Regs., Part II. and the Staff Manual respectively. Title pages will be prepared in manuscript.

WAR DIARY
or
INTELLIGENCE SUMMARY.
(Erase heading not required.)

Army Form C. 2118.

TC/39

Vol 1

16 DIV

1682

Place	Date	Hour	Summary of Events and Information	Remarks and references to Appendices
			War Diary of 9th Bn The Black Watch. for May, 1918. Volume V.	
			4/6/18 [illegible signature] Lt Col. Comdg. 9th Bn The Black Watch.	

D. D. & L., London, E.C.
(A8004) Wt. W1771/M2131 750,000 5/17 Sch. 52 Forms/C2118/14

Instructions regarding War Diaries and Intelligence Summaries are contained in F. S. Regs., Part II. and the Staff Manual respectively. Title pages will be prepared in manuscript.

WAR DIARY

~~INTELLIGENCE SUMMARY.~~

(Erase heading not required.)

Army Form C. 2118.

Place	Date	Hour	Summary of Events and Information	Remarks and references to Appendices
	1.		The re-organizing and distributing of instructors to the three affiliated American Battalions was carried out	
	3.		Lt. D. A. Grant, and 2 Lt. A. Morrison joined the Battalion from 4/5th Bn. The Black Watch to fill vacancies in the establishment.	
	4/10		Training of American Officer and N.C.O. instructors was carried out and the general training and interior economy of the Affiliated American battalions were supervised and rapidly adapted to B.E.F. methods.	
	10.		Lt. D. A. Grant assumed the duties of Adjutant vice 2/Lt. J. Ritchie who assumed command of A. Coy.	
	12.		Gen. Sir Herbert C. O. Plumer, G.C.B., G.C.M.G., G.C.V.O., A.D.C., visited the training area of the 119th Infantry Regiment U.S.N.G. 30th Division (A.E.F.) and inspected the troops at work. 13th Demonstration Platoon of H.A.C., Lt. Pollard V.C. M.C. D.C.M. in command arrived in Louches area.	
	14.		Field Marshal Sir Douglas Haig, K.T., G.C.B., G.C.V.O., K.C.I.E. Commander-in-Chief, British Armies in France, visited the training area of the 30th American Division and inspected the 119th Infantry Regiment U.S.N.G. at work.	
	15.		Lt-Col Sworder, 8th A&SH., Lt-Col Lord Dudley-Gordon, 8/10th Gordon Highlanders and Capt. Christison, 4th Cameron Highlanders conducted over training area preparatory to taking over from O.C. 9th Bn. The Black Watch.	

D. D. & L., London, E.C.
(A10266) Wt W5300/P713 750,000 2/18 Sch. 53 Forms/C2118/16.

Army Form C. 2118.

Instructions regarding War Diaries and Intelligence. Summaries are contained in F. S. Regs., Part II. and the Staff Manual respectively. Title pages will be prepared in manuscript.

WAR DIARY

or

~~INTELLIGENCE SUMMARY.~~

(Erase heading not required.)

Place	Date	Hour	Summary of Events and Information	Remarks and references to Appendices
	16.		Orders were received that the Battalion was being transferred to the 16th Division the following day and was to be transferred to the United Kingdom to be reconstituted	
	17.		The Battalion (less Transport) proceeded by motor lorry to Boulogne, leaving Landrethun at 8-30 A.M. and arriving at Boulogne about noon. The Battalion stayed the night at Ostrohove Camp.	
	18.		The Battalion was transferred to United Kingdom. It embarked at Boulogne about 1-30 P.M. and sailed at 3 P.M. Folkestone was reached about 4-30 P.M. The Battalion entrained, and proceeding from Folkestone arrived about 7 P.M. at Aldershot. About 11 P.M. the Battalion proceeded by march route to Bourley Camp 46, arriving there about 1.30 A.M. on the 19th.	

D. D. & L., London, E.C.
(A10266) Wt W5300/P713 750,000 2/18 Sch. 52 Forms/C2118/16.

Instructions regarding War Diaries and Intelligence Summaries are contained in F. S. Regs., Part II. and the Staff Manual respectively. Title pages will be prepared in manuscript.

WAR DIARY
or
INTELLIGENCE SUMMARY.
(Erase heading not required.)

Army Form C. 2118.

Place	Date	Hour	Summary of Events and Information	Remarks and references to Appendices
	19th		A training nucleus of 8 officers and 51 O R. was selected to proceed to 118th Inf. Bde 39th Division to form training staff for an American Battalion. This personnel was under command of Major (a/Lt Col). J. CRUICKSHANK. The party entrained at BARLIN at 3 30 pm but did not leave until after 10 pm	
	20th		BOULOGNE was reached about 11 am and as the train was not to proceed until evening permission was granted to a proportion of Officers + NCOs to visit BOULOGNE.	
	21st		The party detrained at WATTEN at 6 30 am and proceeded by march route to billets at LA COMMUNE. Breakfast was supplied by the 1/6th Cheshire Regt.	
	22nd		Cleaning of clothing and equipment and smartening up drill were carried out.	
	23rd		At 5 pm the Battalion moved by march route to billets near TOUCHES a distance of some six miles.	
	24/27th		During this period, smartening drill was continued and arrangements were made for the accommodation of an American Battalion in TOUCHES. to be affiliated to 9th Bn. The Black Watch for training.	

D. D. & L., London, E.C.
(A8004) Wt. W1771/M2-31 750,000 5/17 Sch. 52 Forms/C2118/14

Instructions regarding War Diaries and Intelligence Summaries are contained in F. S. Regs., Part II. and the Staff Manual respectively. Title pages will be prepared in manuscript.

WAR DIARY
or
INTELLIGENCE SUMMARY.
(Erase heading not required.)

Army Form C. 2118.

Place	Date	Hour	Summary of Events and Information	Remarks and references to Appendices
	28th		The Battalion moved to new headquarters in IOUCHES. The affiliated American battalion, III/118th Infy Battn. U.S.N.G. (30th Division A.E.F.), detrained at AUDRICQ at 11 30 am and was met by Lt. Col. J CRUICKSHANK, the R.S.M. & 4. C.S.M. The III/118th Infy Battn marched to the billets already arranged for it at IOUCHES, and was affiliated to 9th Bn The Black Watch. For the purpose of training the 9th Black Watch was temporarily attached to the 114th Infy. Brigade (39th Division) but remained under 118th Infy. Brigade for administration.	
	29th		The posting of this Battalion to opposite numbers of the American Unit was carried out.	
	30th		Classes for the training of American N.C.Os. in Musketry and Lewis Gun were commenced.	
	31st		The III/118th Bn. U.S.N.G. left IOUCHES for another area and the 9th Battalion again came under 118th Infy Brigade for training purposes as well as administration. The Battalion moved by march route to billets in IANDRETHUN, and were affiliated to the 2nd & 3rd Battalions 119th Infy. Regt. U.S.N.G. (30th Division A.E.F.). who marched into IANDRETHUN. and YEUSE. between 6pm and 11 pm.	

D. D. & L., London, E.C.
(A8004) Wt. W1771/M2031 750,000 5/17 Sch. 52 Forms/C2118/14

11

16

Instructions regarding War Diaries and Intelligence Summaries are contained in F. S. Regs., Part II. and the Staff Manual respectively. Title pages will be prepared in manuscript.

WAR DIARY
or
~~INTELLIGENCE SUMMARY.~~
(*Erase heading not required.*)

Army Form C. 2118.

Vol 33

Place	Date	Hour	Summary of Events and Information	Remarks and references to Appendices
			9th (S) Btn. The Black Watch, War Diary for June 1918 Volume VI.	
			6-8-18 [signature] Lieut. Col. Commanding 9th (S) Btn. The Black Watch	

D. D. & L., London, E.C.
(A10266) Wt W5300/P713 750,000 2/18 Sch. 52 Forms/C2118/16.

Instructions regarding War Diaries and Intelligence Summaries are contained in F. S. Regs., Part II. and the Staff Manual respectively. Title pages will be prepared in manuscript.

WAR DIARY
or
INTELLIGENCE SUMMARY.
(*Erase heading not required.*)

47 Bde / 16

Army Form C. 2118.

WR 35

Place	Date	Hour	Summary of Events and Information	Remarks and references to Appendices
			Jy 18 Ap 19	
			9th (S) Bn. The Black Watch War Diary for August, 1918. Volume VII.	
			2/9/18 [signature] Lieut. Col. Comdg. 9th (S) Bn. The Black Watch.	B 35

D. D. & L., London, E.C.
(A8004) Wt. W1771/M2-31 750,000 5/17 Sch. 52 Forms/C2118/14

Army Form C. 2118.

Instructions regarding War Diaries and Intelligence Summaries are contained in F. S. Regs., Part II. and the Staff Manual respectively. Title pages will be prepared in manuscript.

WAR DIARY

or

~~INTELLIGENCE SUMMARY.~~

(Erase heading not required.)

Place	Date	Hour	Summary of Events and Information	Remarks and references to Appendices
In the Field	July 30th		The Battalion left BOURLEY CAMP, ALDERSHOT and proceeded by march route to Government Siding, ALDERSHOT, where it entrained for FOLKESTONE. The Battalion moved by two trains one at 12 m.n. and the other at 12.30 a.m. The Battalion detrained at SHORNCLIFFE and marched to rest billets at FOLKESTONE. Tea was served on arrival and breakfast was provided at 7 a.m. The Battalion paraded at 9.50 am and proceeded to embark. BOULOGNE was reached about 2 p.m. and the Battalion proceeded to OSTROHOVE Camp. Not a man fell out on the way.	
	31st		On 31st the Battalion paraded at 4.30 p.m. and proceeded to the station where it entrained for DESVRES. From there the Battalion proceeded by march route to billets in HODICQ. and MUTFLETTE. (Ref. sheet CALAIS 13. 5D. 42.28. and 5D. 60.30.)	
	August 1st		The day was spent in resting and cleaning up.	
	2nd		Training was carried out under Company arrangements. Specialist Classes carried on under their special Officer and N.C.O. Instructors.	
	3rd		Wet weather greatly interfered with the training.	
	4th		Being Sunday, Divine Service was held. Remainder of the day was observed as a day of rest.	
	5th		Training. This included recreational training. Football and inter platoon cross country point to point races were engaged in.	

D. D. & L., London, E.C.
(A8004) Wt. W1771/M2-31 750,000 5/17 Sch. 52 Forms/C2118/14

Instructions regarding War Diaries and Intelligence Summaries are contained in F. S. Regs., Part II. and the Staff Manual respectively. Title pages will be prepared in manuscript.

WAR DIARY
or
~~INTELLIGENCE SUMMARY.~~
(Erase heading not required.)

Army Form C. 2118.

Place	Date	Hour	Summary of Events and Information	Remarks and references to Appendices
	6th		Training was carried out.	
	7th		A + B Coys. carried out firing practices on the range. C + D Coys carried on with general training. The reorganising of the Battalion into the administrative and fighting portions was carried out.	
	10th		About 11 am. orders were received that the 47th Infantry Brigade Group would probably be required to proceed to Fourth Army to collect prisoners. At 11.25 am orders were received that the Battalion would be ready to move in full marching order. Orders were received to stand down ready to move at three hours notice. The Battalion was ready to move at 2.30 pm.	
	11th		The Battalion paraded for Divine Service. About 11.30 am orders were received from 47th Inf Bde. cancelling the move.	
	12th		The Battalion did a route march by companies.	
	13th		The Battalion carried out training according to programme.	
	14th		The Battalion was visited by General. Sir H. S. HORNE, K.C.B., K.C.M.G., Commanding First Army.	
	15th		An officers team of the Battalion played the 14th Bn Leicester Regt at Rugby. & won by 8 points to nil.	

D. D. & L., London, E.C. (A8004) Wt. W1771/M2-31 750,000 5/17 Sch. 52 Forms/C2118/14

Instructions regarding War Diaries and Intelligence Summaries are contained in F. S. Regs., Part II. and the Staff Manual respectively. Title pages will be prepared in manuscript.

WAR DIARY

or

~~INTELLIGENCE SUMMARY~~.

(Erase heading not required.)

Army Form C. 2118.

Place	Date	Hour	Summary of Events and Information	Remarks and references to Appendices
	16th		Orders were received that the Division was to be transferred to the I Corps. Night training was carried out, inter-company reliefs being practised.	
	17th		Training as usual	
	18th		Transport left at 5 PM to proceed by road to the new area. An advance party of the Commanding Officer and Company Commanders left for the new area at 8.30 AM by motor	
	19th		Reveille was at 4.30 A.M. The Battalion paraded ready to embus at 7.10 A.M. The convoy left DOUDEAUVILLE at 8.30 A.M. Some difficulty was experienced owing to the steep nature of the roads. NOEUX-LES-MINES was reached about 4 P.M. and the Battalion moved to billets in BARLIN relieving the 1st Bn. The Black Watch 1st Division. The band of the 1st Battalion played the Battalion into billets.	
	21st		Instructions were received that the Battalion would proceed to the line and occupy the defences at ANNEQUIN in support to 4th Leicester Regt and 8th Welsh Regt in the line HOHENZOLLERN SECTOR (~~[illegible]~~). Battalion proceeded by rail to SAILLY-LA-BOURSE and thence by route march to ANNEQUIN. Battalion Hqrs was in 9 de BETHUNE FOSSE. C Company occupied the VILLAGE LINE and was temporarily under the command of Officer Commanding 18th Bn Welsh Regt.	
	22nd		The Battalion suffered its first casualties when 4 O.R. were wounded by shrapnel. The first fatal casualty was No 25882 PTE FRIZZELL W, D Coy who died of wounds received the same day.	

D. D. & L., London, E.C.
(A10266) Wt W5300/P713 750,000 2/18 Sch. 52 Forms/C2118/16.

Instructions regarding War Diaries and Intelligence Summaries are contained in F. S. Regs., Part II. and the Staff Manual respectively. Title pages will be prepared in manuscript.

WAR DIARY
or
~~INTELLIGENCE SUMMARY~~.
(Erase heading not required.)

Army Form C. 2118.

Place	Date	Hour	Summary of Events and Information	Remarks and references to Appendices
	25th		D. Coy relieved C Coy in the VILLAGE LINE.	
	24th		The Battalion moved to the front line and relieved the Right Battalion (1[illegible]th Welsh Regt). A & C. Coys were in the front line. B & D. Coys were in support. One Coy of the 18th Bn Welsh Regt was holding the Village Line and was under temporary command of this Battalion.	
	28/31.		Holding the line. Situation generally quiet. Some gas shelling was experienced and occasional bursts of heavy artillery fire. Constant patrolling was carried out as the enemy was believed to be retiring on our front. Capt F. PROUDFOOT, M.C. joined the Battalion on 25th inst. During the period the Battalion had ten casualties, two of which were fatal	

D. D. & L., London, E.C.
(A10266) Wt W5300/P713 750,000 2/18 Sch. 52 Forms/C2118/16.

Instructions regarding War Diaries and Intelligence Summaries are contained in F. S. Regs., Part II. and the Staff Manual respectively. Title pages will be prepared in manuscript.

WAR DIARY
or
INTELLIGENCE SUMMARY.
(*Erase heading not required.*)

Army Form C. 2118.

VR 36

B 36

Place	Date	Hour	Summary of Events and Information	Remarks and references to Appendices
			9th (S) Btn. The Black Watch War Diary for September 1918 Volume VIII Alan Stewart Major, Commanding 9th (S) Btn The Black Watch 3/10/18	

D. D. & L., London, E.C.
(A10266) Wt W5300/P713 750,000 2/18 Sch. 52 Forms/C2118/16.

Instructions regarding War Diaries and Intelligence Summaries are contained in F. S. Regs., Part II. and the Staff Manual respectively. Title pages will be prepared in manuscript.

WAR DIARY
or
~~INTELLIGENCE~~ SUMMARY.
(*Erase heading not required.*)

Army Form C. 2118.

Place	Date	Hour	Summary of Events and Information	Remarks and references to Appendices
	1918 Sept. 1		The enemy attempted to raid one of our posts on "C" Coy front but was successfully driven off leaving two prisoners in our hands. We suffered only one casualty (wounded). "B" & "D" Coys relieved "A" & "C" Coys in the line. "B" Coy on the right flank and "D" Coy on the left. "C" Coy became Right support Coy and "A" Coy left support Coy.	
	2.		Instructions were received early in the morning to send out four fighting patrols to establish posts in the enemy 2nd line. Two patrols from "A" Coy under 2/Lt A. C. Robertson and 2/Lt C. R. Belford and two patrols from "C" Coy under 2/Lt C. M. Humphries and 2/Lt H. F. K. Wedderburn left our trenches at 4-30 a.m. and proceeded towards the enemy lines. The Commanding Officer moved up to RAILWAY KEEP to receive reports from the patrol leaders. No reports came in up to 6-15 a.m. and at this period the advanced Hqrs moved up to Right Front Coy Hqrs. The first reports came in about 10-5 a.m. stating one patrol had been held up by the enemy and the remainder had lost direction and had returned but would proceed out again. There were 31 casualties this includes killed, wounded and missing. 2/Lt C. R. Belford, missing believed killed.	

D. D. & L., London, E.C.
(A10266) Wt W5300/P713 750,000 2/18 Sch. 52 Forms/C2118/16.

Army Form C. 2118.

WAR DIARY
~~or~~
~~INTELLIGENCE SUMMARY.~~
(*Erase heading not required.*)

Instructions regarding War Diaries and Intelligence Summaries are contained in F. S. Regs., Part II. and the Staff Manual respectively. Title pages will be prepared in manuscript.

Place	Date	Hour	Summary of Events and Information	Remarks and references to Appendices
	3/5.		Holding the line. Constant patrolling. Enemy reported to have evacuated FOSSE Trench Large fires seen behind enemy lines. "B" & "D" Coys heavy casualties. 60, nearly all gas cases. 2/Lt. M. Lambroughton was gassed on 5th.	
	6.		Pushed forward and occupied post in FOSSE TRENCH. Patrols reconnoitred ground between FOSSE TRENCH and Railway. These outposts were in position at 9 a.m. Enemy counter attacked at 4 p.m and drove our posts in. They [illegible] on to our old front line. Casualties were fairly heavy. 49 killed, wounded and gassed. Two Coys of the 18th Welsh came up to relieve, but occupied the Reserve line and VILLAGE LINES. They did very good work in helping to bring in the killed and wounded.	
	7.		Relieved by 18th Welsh and proceeded to billets in NOEUX LES MINES.	
	8/11		Cleaning up and resting. Baths for Battalion on 9th. C/O gave lecture and Battalion watched a demonstration by B. Coy on Battle platoon patrols advancing by bounds. Parades under Company arrangements.	
	12.		Relieved 18th Welsh in HOHENZOLLERN SECTOR (NORTH), Right sub-sector, left Battalion relief starting at 2 p.m. Took over advanced posts. B H Q moved up to RAILWAY KEEP at 10 p.m. About 30 gas shells on our front	

D. D. & L., London, E.C.
(A10266) Wt W5300/P713 750,000 2/18 Sch. 52 Forms/C2118/16.

Instructions regarding War Diaries and Intelligence Summaries are contained in F. S. Regs., Part II. and the Staff Manual respectively. Title pages will be prepared in manuscript.

WAR DIARY
~~or~~
~~INTELLIGENCE SUMMARY.~~
(*Erase heading not required.*)

Army Form C. 2118.

Place	Date	Hour	Summary of Events and Information	Remarks and references to Appendices
	13		"A" & "C" Coys pushed forward and occupied positions at A29a 45.50 A29a 35.60 A29c 50.70. A29c 60.70. A.29c 40.35. A 29c 80.10. Battn Hqrs moved at 4 a.m. to MUNSTER TUNNEL	
	14.		Another advance by the battalion. They now occupy position along the road running NORTH and SOUTH between CORONS DE PEKIN and AUCHY. "A" & "C" Coys occupying these positions at 9 P.M. "B" & "D" Coys relieved "A" & "C" in the front position. 2/Lt W.D.G. Reid, 2/Lt E.R.C. Walker and 2/Lt J.H. Lauder went to hospital suffering from gas poisoning. High concentration of gas round our forward posts	
	15.		2/Lt C.R. Belford's body found. Now reported killed in action. 2/Lt J. McClure left our lines with a patrol to reconnoitre ground between outposts and GIBBON TRENCH. Holding the line. Everything quiet.	
	16.		Holding the line. The enemy occasionally shelled FOSSE 8 and LES BRIQUES. Were relieved at 7-30 p.m. by the 18th Welsh. B.H.Q moved from MUNSTER TUNNEL to old B.H.Q underneath the railway. Companies came back to - "A" Coy HENLEY POST, "B" Coy GLOSTER POST, "C" Coy ANNEQUIN and D Coy to SUSSEX TRENCH. Enemy aeroplane dropped 6 bombs outside Brigade Hqrs	
	17.		Everything very quiet. Men went for baths to ANNEQUIN.	

D. D. & L., London, E.C.
(A10266) Wt W5300/P713 750,000 2/18 Sch. 52 Forms/C2118/16.

Instructions regarding War Diaries and Intelligence Summaries are contained in F. S. Regs., Part II. and the Staff Manual respectively. Title pages will be prepared in manuscript.

WAR DIARY

~~or~~

~~INTELLIGENCE SUMMARY.~~

(Erase heading not required.)

Army Form C. 2118.

Place	Date	Hour	Summary of Events and Information	Remarks and references to Appendices
	18.		"C" Coy went from ANNEQUIN and occupied CENTRAL KEEP relieving a Coy Coy of the Scottish Rifles. Lieut D A Grant proceeded to details for a rest. 2/Lt. C Webster took over Adjutant. Heavy shelling on our right. Capt D. K. Hamilton joined battalion and took over command of "C" Coy	
	19.		Holding the line. Hqrs in RAILWAY Embankment. Very quiet	
	20.		Relieved 18th Welsh at 9 PM. Headquarters in RAILWAY KEEP. A few Gas Shell round FOSSE 8. Heavy shelling in sector on our Right.	
	21		Holding the line. Very quiet on our front. Battn Hqrs moved to EVENING POST. "A" Coy relieved in Left Front by the 34th London Regt. Pte J Duncan "A" Coy received the Military Medal	
	22.		Relieved by the 9th Royal Scots. Embussed at SAILLY LABOURSE and proceeded to HESDIGNEUL. Men are billeted in old Aerodrome	
	23/24		Parades under Coy arrangements	
	25		Demonstration: Infantry and Tanks in advance	
	26		Capt D K Kirk took over Command of Battalion.	

D. D. & L., London, E.C.
(A10266) Wt W5300/P713 750,000 2/18 Sch. 52 Forms/C2118/16.

Instructions regarding War Diaries and Intelligence Summaries are contained in F. S. Regs., Part II. and the Staff Manual respectively. Title pages will be prepared in manuscript.

WAR DIARY

~~or~~

~~INTELLIGENCE SUMMARY.~~

(Erase heading not required.)

Army Form C. 2118.

Place	Date	Hour	Summary of Events and Information	Remarks and references to Appendices
	27.		Major A. J. Stewart of 4/5th Bn. The Black Watch took over Command of Battn from Capt. D. K. Kirk	
	28/29		Parades under Coy arrangements	
	30.		Lecture by Tank Commander on co-operation between Tanks and Infantry in advance	

D. D. & L., London, E.C.
(A10266) Wt W5300/P713 750,000 2/18 Sch. 52 Forms/C2118/16.

47/6

Army Form C. 2118.

Instructions regarding War Diaries and Intelligence Summaries are contained in F. S. Regs., Part II. and the Staff Manual respectively. Title pages will be prepared in manuscript.

WAR DIARY

~~or~~

~~INTELLIGENCE SUMMARY.~~

(Erase heading not required.)

Place	Date	Hour	Summary of Events and Information	Remarks and references to Appendices
			Vol 40	
			9th (S) Btn. The Black Watch War Diary for October 1918. Volume IX	B37
			9th (S) BN. THE BLACK WATCH No. B.W. 677 DATE 2-11-18 ORDERLY ROOM	
			Ah. J. Stewart Lieut-Col. Commdg 9th (S) Bn The Black Watch	

D. D. & L., London, E.C.
(A10266) Wt W5300/P713 750,000 2/18 Sch. 52 Forms/C2118/16.

Instructions regarding War Diaries and Intelligence Summaries are contained in F. S. Regs., Part II. and the Staff Manual respectively. Title pages will be prepared in manuscript.

WAR DIARY

or

~~INTELLIGENCE SUMMARY.~~

(Erase heading not required.)

Army Form C. 2118.

Place	Date	Hour	Summary of Events and Information	Remarks and references to Appendices
	1.		Training at HESDIGNEUL	
			Lieut F. W. F. Whitehead reported for duty on 30-9-18 and was posted to A Co.	
			2/Lt C. L. S. Pattullo rejoined from hospital	
	2.		Training.	
			2/Lt J. Ritchie transferred from A to C. Coy.	
			2/Lt F. W. Bedford transferred from C to A Coy.	
	3.		Training	
			2/Lt A. W. Macdonald granted leave to U.K. 3-10-18 to 17-10-18.	
	4.		Training.	
	5.		Training	
			The following officers reported for duty	
			Lieut W. Reid — B Coy	
			Lieut J. H. Morton — C "	
			2/Lt J. Wishart — A "	
	6.		Training.	
			Lt-Col J. Cruickshank granted leave to U.K. 7-10-18 to 21-10-18	
	7.		~~Rat~~	

D. D. & L., London, E.C.
(A10266) Wt W5300/P713 750,000 2/18 Sch. 52 Forms/C2118/16.

2

Instructions regarding War Diaries and Intelligence Summaries are contained in F. S. Regs., Part II. and the Staff Manual respectively. Title pages will be prepared in manuscript.

WAR DIARY

~~or~~

~~INTELLIGENCE SUMMARY.~~

(Erase heading not required.)

Army Form C. 2118.

Place	Date	Hour	Summary of Events and Information	Remarks and references to Appendices
	7.		Lieut J. Cochrane reported for duty and was posted to A. Coy 2/Lt R.J. Cameron reported for duty and was posted to D. Coy Capt A.K. Hamilton took over the duties of Adjutant from Lieut G.C. Gray	
	8.		The Battalion proceeded by route march to ANNEQUIN and relieved the 18th Gloucester Regt as Battn of Brigade in reserve. Battn HQ for the night was in ANNEQUIN FOSSE.	

D. D. & L., London, E.C.
(A10266) Wt W5300/P713 750,000 2/18 Sch. 52 Forms/C2118/16.

Instructions regarding War Diaries and Intelligence Summaries are contained in F. S. Regs., Part II. and the Staff Manual respectively. Title pages will be prepared in manuscript.

WAR DIARY

OF

~~INTELLIGENCE SUMMARY.~~

(Erase heading not required.)

Army Form C. 2118.

3

Place	Date	Hour	Summary of Events and Information	Remarks and references to Appendices
	9.		The Battn moved from ANNEQUIN and relieved 22nd North[umberland] Fusiliers in Brigade Reserve. The Battn was located in the [illegible] of the O. B. L. [illegible] in front of CAMBRIN. The front line at this time was the line of the HAUTE DEULE Canal Leicesters went into the line Welsh went into support (Note – One Battn of the 16th Divn in the line) The march was 1¾ miles	
	10.		No change. Coys worked at collecting salvage A [illegible] rifle range was constructed in one of the [illegible] in the old "No man's Land". Lieut. [illegible] Brown was admitted to Hospital A draft of 12 O.R.s reported for duty	
	11.		No change. Coys worked at collecting salvage and did some [illegible] A draft of 17 O.R.s reported for duty	
	12.		No change. The Battn received great praise for the great amount of salvage collected during this period in Bde reserve. 2/Lt. H. [illegible] Davies, 11th Hants was taken on strength and posted to [illegible] Coy	

D. D. & L., London, E.C.
(A10266) Wt W5300/P713 750,000 2/18 Sch. 52 Forms/C2118/16.

Instructions regarding War Diaries and Intelligence Summaries are contained in F. S. Regs., Part II. and the Staff Manual respectively. Title pages will be prepared in manuscript.

WAR DIARY

~~or~~

~~INTELLIGENCE SUMMARY.~~

(*Erase heading not required.*)

Army Form C. 2118.

4

Place	Date	Hour	Summary of Events and Information	Remarks and references to Appendices
	13		The Black Watch relieved the Welsh in the Battle Zone. H.Q. Cité de Douvrin B Coy in DOUVRIN (R. Front) D Coy (L. Front) A Coy HAISNES (R. Support) C Coy (L Support) The Welsh relieved the Leicesters in the front line. The Battn marched via AUCHY and HAISNES 3½ miles Warning instructions were issued as to action in case of an enemy retirement which was considered imminent.	
	14		This day it was ascertained that the enemy had withdrawn from his position on the [illegible] bank and the Welsh crossed the canal without opposition using two small [illegible] each of which only held 4 men at one time. The Welsh then established bridge heads on the eastern side of canal and during the evening the R.E. threw across a light foot-bridge capable of taking one man at a time. During the early part of the night the Black Watch passed through the Welsh and took up an outpost line running N & S between BAUVIN and PROVIN with 3 Coys. B & D in front and A Coy in support. Battn H.Q. was in the Dynamite Factory near [illegible]. During the night orders were received for the Battn to advance and take up the general line ALLENNES (exclusive) to CARVIN (inclusive). This operation commenced at dawn on 15-10-18. Distance marched this day 2 miles.	

D. D. & L., London, E.C.
(A10266) Wt W5300/P713 750,000 2/18 Sch. 52 Forms/C2118/16.

5

Instructions regarding War Diaries and Intelligence Summaries are contained in F. S. Regs., Part II. and the Staff Manual respectively. Title pages will be prepared in manuscript.

WAR DIARY

~~or~~

~~INTELLIGENCE SUMMARY.~~

(Erase heading not required.)

Army Form C. 2118.

Place	Date	Hour	Summary of Events and Information	Remarks and references to Appendices
	15.		The Battalion advanced with B. Coy (R) and D. Coy (L) in front. C. Coy in support. A. Coy in reserve. The Battalion was responsible for the whole of the divisional front. The operation was completely successful the only opposition being an occasional sniper. Two prisoners were captured by B Coy near CARVIN. Touch was maintained throughout with the 15th Division on the Right and the 58th Division on the left. D. Coy had 1 casualty. Battn HQ moved up to ANNOEULLIN and afterwards to CARVIN. About 1400 orders were received to push forward to the line CHEMY – CARVIN (the latter inclusive). C (Left) and A (Right) advanced through D & B Coys but were met with heavy machine gun fire and were unable to move far forward. At nightfall however A Coy sent a patrol through [illegible] and when this patrol returned and reported the village clear of the enemy a platoon post was established on the [illegible]. Capt (a/Major) A. J. Stewart DSO appointed Lt Col on assuming command of the Battn 27-9-18 The distance covered this day was 4½ miles.	
	16.		At 0630 the Battalion continued the advance with two companies front B Coy Right, D. Coy Left. No resistance was met with and the Right Coy occupied their objective which included PHALEMPIN and reported this at 0830.	(cont)

D. D. & L., London, E.C.
(A10266) Wt W5300/P713 750,000 2/18 Sch. 52 Forms/C2118/16.

6

Army Form C. 2118.

Instructions regarding War Diaries and Intelligence Summaries are contained in F. S. Regs., Part II. and the Staff Manual respectively. Title pages will be prepared in manuscript.

WAR DIARY

~~or~~

~~INTELLIGENCE SUMMARY.~~

(Erase heading not required.)

Place	Date	Hour	Summary of Events and Information	Remarks and references to Appendices
	16 (Contd)		Owing to the 55th Division on our left not being forward, a defensive flank was formed by the left front Coy and the left support Coy. At 0930 Patrols reported the ground as far as the [illegible] on the left to be clear of the enemy. At 1100 the 55th Division moved forward through GONDECOURT and our left going forward in touch with them reached the objective. The progress of this operation was reported at H.Q. At 1400 the left front Coy had established [illegible] the east of WATTESSART(?) and were in touch with the Right front Coy. The [illegible] passed through our outpost line in the evening and took up a line which included MARTINSART(?) and ATTILLES(?). During the day the Battalion [illegible] the first [illegible] villages in which the inhabitants were still living. Our men had a great reception. Batt. H.Q. for the night was at WACHEMY(?) Major R. McKean(?) reported for duty from 5th Camerons. Distance covered this day 2½ miles.	
	17		This day the 16th Division continued the advance. The 47th Bde acted as advanced guard to the Division. The [illegible] and [illegible] with other units formed the vanguard. The Main Guard consisted of Commander Lt-Col Brown(?) D.S.O. M.C. 47th Inf Bde H.Q. 3 Coys (A, B & C) 9th Black Watch – Coy H.Q. and 2 secs M.G.C. – 180th Bde R.F.A. less 2 secs. 18 pdrs. 1 sec 6" Newtons – Bearer sec 111 Fd. Ambce – Echelon B. 47th Bde transport. 1 Coy (D) 9th Black Watch – 1 sec 60 pdrs. – 116th R.G.A. (Contd)	

D. D. & L., London, E.C.
(A10266) Wt W5300/P713 750,000 2/18 Sch. 52 Forms/C2118/16.

7

Army Form C. 2118.

WAR DIARY
or
~~INTELLIGENCE SUMMARY~~.
(Erase heading not required.)

Instructions regarding War Diaries and Intelligence Summaries are contained in F. S. Regs., Part II. and the Staff Manual respectively. Title pages will be prepared in manuscript.

Place	Date	Hour	Summary of Events and Information	Remarks and references to Appendices
	17 (contd)		The route followed by the Battn was through ATTICHES - TREURE - PONT-A-MARC, these villages having been cleared of the enemy by the vanguard. The Bn spent the night in defensive positions round LA PLANQUE. Battn H.Q. spent the night in PONT A MARC. The outpost line included TEMPLEUVE where some opposition had been met with from enemy M.Gs. Distance covered this day 4½ miles.	
	18.		The advance was continued with the Welsh and [illegible] as vanguard. The Black Watch marched through TEMPLEUVE and took up [illegible] round the Eastern outskirts of this town, where they spent the night. Battn HQ was in TEMPLEUVE for the night. Distance covered this day 2½ miles.	
	19.		The advance continued with the Welsh as vanguard. The villages of BACHY, SENTIER, RUMES and TAIN-IRVIES were secured and the Black Watch moving through these places by route march reached the FLORENT area where they spent the night. Battn H.Q. was in CHATEAU des DOMINICAINS. The Battn covered 10,000 yards this day.	

D. D. & L., London, E.C.
(A10266) Wt W5300/P713 750,000 2/18 Sch. 52 Forms/C2118/16.

Instructions regarding War Diaries and Intelligence Summaries are contained in F. S. Regs., Part II. and the Staff Manual respectively. Title pages will be prepared in manuscript.

WAR DIARY

~~or~~

~~INTELLIGENCE SUMMARY.~~

(Erase heading not required.)

Army Form C. 2118.

8

Place	Date	Hour	Summary of Events and Information	Remarks and references to Appendices
	20.		In the early morning the Black Watch advanced through the outpost line and on a two Coy front (A Coy Right – D Coy left) with B Coy in Support and C Coy in reserve. The objective was a line E of MONT de la JUSTICE and E of ST MAUR. The Right Coy gained its objective easily but the left Coy D met with considerable resistance from M.G. fire in the wood S.W. of ST MAUR and in ST MAUR itself. This opposition was overcome and the Coy was able to occupy its objective in the afternoon. 2 Battn runners and 1 man of D Coy were killed this day and 5 men of D Coy wounded. It was obvious that the enemy's resistance was stiffening. The two front Coys dug in on their objective and B Coy and C Coy dug in in support and reserve positions respectively. Battn HQ was established in a farm at U.21.d.6.3. The enemy's artillery showed much increased activity during the day and night, shelling our advanced troops and roads in rear. The night passed without incident except for enemy shelling. Various patrols were sent out to try to reach the SCHELDT River but all were prevented from doing this by enemy M.G. fire.	

D. D. & L., London, E.C.
(A10266) Wt W5300/P713 750,000 2/18 Sch. 52 Forms/C2118/16.

9

Instructions regarding War Diaries and Intelligence Summaries are contained in F. S. Regs., Part II. and the Staff Manual respectively. Title pages will be prepared in manuscript.

WAR DIARY
~~or~~
~~INTELLIGENCE SUMMARY.~~
(Erase heading not required.)

Army Form C. 2118.

Place	Date	Hour	Summary of Events and Information	Remarks and references to Appendices
	21.		Coys remained in the positions which they had dug in the previous day. Capt Proudfoot M.C. and a sergeant of A Coy carried out a patrol into BRUYELLE in the forenoon and found this village occupied by the enemy. This patrol shot two Germans and returned. In the afternoon an officers patrol from B. Coy reconnoitred the same village and were met with considerable M.G. and rifle fire. In the evening the Battn was relieved by the Leicesters. The relief went smoothly and D & A Coys proceeded to billets in TAINTIGNIES, B. Coy to LONGUESAULT, C Coy to ST. MAUR. Battn H.Q. was in TAINTIGNIES.	
	22.		No change A draft of 35 O.R.s joined the Battn. The 4/5th [illegible] were billeted in the next village L'ECUELLE.	
	23.		No change A draft of 14 O.R. joined the Battn	
	24		No change 2 men of C Coy and 5 men of B Coy were wounded by shell fire at LONGUESAULT 2/Lt E. R. C. Walker reported for duty and was posted to A. Coy	

D. D. & L., London, E.C.
(A10266) Wt W5300/P713 750,000 2/18 Sch. 52 Forms/C2118/16.

10

Instructions regarding War Diaries and Intelligence Summaries are contained in F. S. Regs., Part II. and the Staff Manual respectively. Title pages will be prepared in manuscript.

WAR DIARY

or

~~INTELLIGENCE SUMMARY~~.

(Erase heading not required.)

Army Form C. 2118.

Place	Date	Hour	Summary of Events and Information	Remarks and references to Appendices
	25.		The 47th Bde was relieved in the evening by the 49th Bde. The 34th London Regt relieved the 9th Black Watch. The relief went smoothly. The B.W. proceeded on relief to billets in SENTIER. 1 man was wounded.	
	26.		No change. Half of the Battn spent the day cleaning up. 2 coys worked on roads. 2/Lt. E. R. C. Walker was transferred from A. to B. Coy. 2/Lt Y. W. Dundas reported for duty and was posted to B. Coy 2/Lt. A. J. G. Loxton took over Signalling Officer's duties from 2/Lt. J. L. Adams. Lt W. Reid took over P.M.C. from 2/Lt C. Webster. Sgt. Paton took over Mess Sgt. from L/Cpl Scott A draft of 5 O.R's reported for duty.	
	27.		Sunday – Church parade was held at SENTIER	
	28/31		Training was carried out. Working parties were supplied to work under R.E's. repairing roads. Lieut A. D. McDearmid reported for duty on 31st and was posted to C Coy 2/Lt J. W. Hill reported for duty on 31st and was posted to B. Coy.	

D. D. & L., London, E.C.
(A10266) Wt W5300/P713 750,000 2/18 Sch. 52 Forms/C2118/16.

Operation Order No. 23.

Ref. Sheets 44 & 44A

1. 4) Inf. Bde. will continue to advance at 0730 today with 9th Division on the right and [illegible] on the left.

2. Right Bdy. will be [illegible] F21 c 5.5. A10 c 7.7. A6 a 5.5.
Left Bdy. with 5th [illegible] [illegible] line [illegible] E from F4 a 0.9.

3. Objective line of River Running through A2 central and A8 1066. Final objective. E of CORRIEUX E of BOIS DE CYSOING. E of BOIS de la TASSONNIERE.

4. Order of March Inf. B.B.C. D.A. Transport.
Bn. will be ready to move forward by 0800.
Starting point being Rd Junction in F14 b 5.4.
~~Rendezvous~~ at starting point 0800

0550
19.10.18.

[illegible signature]
Capt & Adj.

(1) ADVANCE PARTIES

1 officer + 1 NCO HQ + 1 officer + NCO per platoon will report at these HQrs at 1100.

Capt. R. Phelps will be in charge of advance party.

T.O. will send an NCO to SENTIER to take over transport lines.

TRANSPORT

(2) 1. Echelon "B" will rejoin 1st line transport by 1200.

2. All transport details less 4 Coy L.G. limbers and Coy cookers, water cart & officers mess cart will move to new area at 1400.

3. ~~4~~ 8 Coy L.G. limbers will report at Coy HQrs LONGUE SAULT at 1830.

(4) PLATOON, 1st Corps Cyclists on relief will be attached to 34th London Regt. & will draw rations from the 34th London Regt from the 25th.

(9) Dispositions, Defence schemes & battle positions will be carefully handed over.

Coys must take the greatest care to hand over billets thoroughly clean & that proper latrines are made.

(10) Completion of relief to be reported as coys pass HQrs.

On arrival in new billets coys will send a runner to report "all in" & to remain at HQrs.

T28, c, 3, 7

SECRET   Copy No.

9th Black Watch RO

24th 10-18

Reference map - sheet 37.

1. 47th Inf Bde will be relieved by the 48 Inf Bde on October 25th.

2. BATTALION RELIEF

(A) The 9th Black Watch will be relieved by the 34th London Regt in the evening of the 25th inst. The London Regt relieving the corresponding Coys.

(B) GUIDES

A & D Coys no guides
B " 1 guide per platoon at Coy HQ at 1830
C " 5 guides at B Coy HQrs at 1830
B & C Coys 34th London Regt will be guided up to "B" Coy HQrs LONGUE SAULT by Bn. Guides who will meet incoming Coys at their HQrs at 1800

(C) COY RELIEF

Coys will march back to SENTIER T.28, a & c.

ROUTE TANTIGNIES - FLORENT - TRACK in T.30, b, & a & 29 b. to Main Rd at T.29 b.00.99 thence via RUMES to SENTIER.

ORDER ~~HQ~~ HQrs. D, A, B & C Coys.

GUIDES will meet Coys at T.28, a. 3.7 & guide them to billets.

Instructions regarding War Diaries and Intelligence Summaries are contained in F. S. Regs., Part II. and the Staff Manual respectively. Title pages will be prepared in manuscript.

WAR DIARY
or
~~INTELLIGENCE SUMMARY.~~
(Erase heading not required.)

Army Form C. 2118.

VR 41

Place	Date	Hour	Summary of Events and Information	Remarks and references to Appendices
			9th (S). Btn. The Black Watch War Diary for November 1918. Volume X	

9th (S) BN. THE BLACK WATCH
No. BW848
DATE 1-12-18
ORDERLY ROOM

B 38

Aln. J Stewart Lieut-Col
Commanding 9th (S) Battn The Black Watch.

D. D. & L., London, E.C.
(A10266) Wt W5300/P713 750,000 2/18 Sch. 52 Forms/C2118/16.

Instructions regarding War Diaries and Intelligence Summaries are contained in F. S. Regs., Part II. and the Staff Manual respectively. Title pages will be prepared in manuscript.

WAR DIARY
or
INTELLIGENCE SUMMARY.
(Erase heading not required.)

Army Form C. 2118.

Place	Date	Hour	Summary of Events and Information	Remarks and references to Appendices
	1.		Coys continued training at SENTIER 5 O.R's evac sick Lt-Col A. J. Stewart D.S.O proceeded on leave to U.K. Capt. J. R PHILIP M.C took over command of the Battalion	
	2.		Coys continued training at SENTIER 2 O.R's evac sick	
	3.		The 9th Black Watch moved to ESCOEUILS Area taking up Billets vacated by 18th Scottish Rifles. Battn HQ and C & D Coys. in WACHEMY. Very scattered billets 2 O.R's joined the Battalion 3 O.R's evacuated sick.	I
	4.		The Coys commenced training in ESCOEUILS and WACHEMY Areas 14 O.R's joined the Battalion 1 O.R. evacuated sick 1. O.R to M. Inf. Base Depot (unfit)	
	5.		The Coys continued training in ESCOEUILS and WACHEMY Areas. 2/Lt. J. R McCallum rejoined the Battalion and was posted to "B" Coy	

D. D. & L., London, E.C.
(A10266) Wt W5300/P713 750,000 2/18 Sch. 52 Forms/C2118/16.

Instructions regarding War Diaries and Intelligence Summaries are contained in F. S. Regs., Part II. and the Staff Manual respectively. Title pages will be prepared in manuscript.

WAR DIARY
or
INTELLIGENCE SUMMARY.
(Erase heading not required.)

Army Form C. 2118.

Place	Date	Hour	Summary of Events and Information	Remarks and references to Appendices
	6.		Coys carried on training in ESCOEUILS and WACHEMY Areas. 1 man died of wounds on 3/11/18.	
	7		Coys carried on training in ESCOEUILS and WACHEMY Areas 2 O.R's joined the Battalion 2 O.R's evacuated sick	
	8.		Coys carried on training in ESCOEUILS and WACHEMY Areas 5 O.R's joined the Battalion 1 man died of Influenza 5/11/18	
	9.		Coys carried on training in their respective Areas in ESCOEUILS and WACHEMY. 1 O.R. joined the Battalion 2. O.R's evacuated sick	
	10		Battalion moved to area left of TAINTIGNIES. Battn H.Q. and B. Coy in LE PREAU. C + D. Coys in BOURGAGE. A Coy in LONGUE SAULTE 2/Lt W. D. G. REID rejoined the Battalion and was posted to B. Coy	II

D. D. & L., London, E.C.
(A10266) Wt W5300/P713 750,000 2/18 Sch. 52 Forms/C2118/16.

Instructions regarding War Diaries and Intelligence Summaries are contained in F. S. Regs., Part II. and the Staff Manual respectively. Title pages will be prepared in manuscript.

WAR DIARY

~~or~~

~~INTELLIGENCE SUMMARY.~~

(Erase heading not required.)

Army Form C. 2118.

Place	Date	Hour	Summary of Events and Information	Remarks and references to Appendices
	11.		Message came by 'phone from Division that Hostilities ceased at 1100 hours today. The band accordingly paraded and played outside Battn H Q where an eightsome reel was formed by the officers present. During the dancing the Divisional General arrived and congratulated the Battn. on the successful termination of the War and wished it luck in the future. The Brigadier General arrived later and added his congratulations. The band eventually visited the Coys and reels were danced by officers and men. In spite of a thin drizzle which set in late in the afternoon a bonfire was lit directly darkness set in. The whole Battalion was present. Several reels were danced to the light of red ground flares and very lights. The first Peace Operation Order was received from Brigade at 1830 hours. The only thing which marred the general rejoicings was the fact that there was a complete absence of whiskey in the Battalion.	
	12.		Coys remained in LE PREAU. Games and recreational training were carried out during the day. 2/Lt. E. R. C. WALKER admitted to hospital 10-11-18.	

D. D. & L., London, E.C.
(A10266) Wt W5300/P713 750,000 2/18 Sch. 52 Forms/C2118/16.

Instructions regarding War Diaries and Intelligence Summaries are contained in F. S. Regs., Part II. and the Staff Manual respectively. Title pages will be prepared in manuscript.

WAR DIARY
or
~~INTELLIGENCE SUMMARY.~~
(Erase heading not required.)

Army Form C. 2118.

Place	Date	Hour	Summary of Events and Information	Remarks and references to Appendices
	13.		Coys still in LE PREAU Area. Recreational training carried on during the day. 9 O.R's joined the Battalion 3. O.R's evacuated sick Lt C.M. HUMPHRIES transferred to U.K 24-10-18. 2/Lt. H.L. BIRRELL transferred to U.K. 31-10-18.	
	14.		Coys still in LE PREAU Area. After inspection of billets and men to ensure cleanliness, games were played for the remainder of the day. 5 O.R's joined the Battalion 2 O.R's evacuated sick. LT J.M. BROWN transferred to U.K. sick 5-11-18.	
	15.		Battalion moved to COBRIEUX Area. B & C. Coys in LA POSTERIE A & B. Coys in COBRIEUX Battn H.Q in CHATEAU DU FAY.	III
	16.		Battalion moved to AVELIN Area. Battn H.Q. in CHATEAU DES ROTOURS. 2/Lt W.D.G. REID. transferred from B. to C. Coy. 2/Lt. D.R.R. BURT transferred from C ~~to B~~. Coy.	IV

D. D. & L., London, E.C.
(A10266) Wt W5300/P713 750,000 2/18 Sch. 52 Forms/C2118/16.

Instructions regarding War Diaries and Intelligence Summaries are contained in F. S. Regs., Part II. and the Staff Manual respectively. Title pages will be prepared in manuscript.

WAR DIARY
or
INTELLIGENCE SUMMARY.
(Erase heading not required.)

Army Form C. 2118.

Place	Date	Hour	Summary of Events and Information	Remarks and references to Appendices
	17.		Battalion carried out training in AVELIN 14 O.R's joined 5. O.R's evacuated sick	
	18		Battalion continued training in AVELIN. 9. OR's joined 1 O.R. evacuated sick. 3. O.R's to M. Inf. Base Depot (unfit)	
	19		Battalion continued training in AVELIN. 10 O.R's joined 1. O.R evacuated sick	
	20.		Lt-Col A.J. STEWART, D.S.O. returned from leave to U.K. and took over command of the Battalion Coys carried on training in AVELIN 1 O.R. joined 1 O.R. proceeded to 47th T.M. Battery.	
	21.		Battalion trained in AVELIN AREA 2. O.R's joined 2 O.R's evacuated sick	

D. D. & L., London, E.C.
(A10266) Wt W5300/P713 750,000 2/18 Sch. 52 Forms/C2118/16.

Army Form C. 2118.

WAR DIARY
or
~~INTELLIGENCE SUMMARY.~~
(*Erase heading not required.*)

Instructions regarding War Diaries and Intelligence Summaries are contained in F. S. Regs., Part II. and the Staff Manual respectively. Title pages will be prepared in manuscript.

Place	Date	Hour	Summary of Events and Information	Remarks and references to Appendices
	22.		Battalion trained in AVELIN Area 1 O.R. joined. S/43484 Pte GIBSON, K. taken on strength from 4/5th Black Watch and promoted Sgt. Drummer. 2. O.R's evacuated sick.	
	23.		Battalion trained in AVELIN 5 O.R's joined.	
	24		Coy training in AVELIN Area Lieut F.L. McGRADY taken on strength from 4/5th Black Watch from 23-11-18. 5 O.R's evacuated sick.	
	25		Coys carried on training in AVELIN. Major. R McLEAN, 6th Camerons (attached), transferred to 15th Division	
	26		Coys carried on training in AVELIN 2/Lt. H.L. BIRRELL taken on strength 6 O.R's joined. 1 man died while on leave to U.K.	
	27.		Battalion moved to FRETIN Area Battn. H.Q. in CHATEAU DE FRETIN.	V

D. D. & L., London, E.C.
(A10266) Wt W5300/P713 750,000 2/18 Sch. 52 Forms/C2118/16.

Instructions regarding War Diaries and Intelligence Summaries are contained in F. S. Regs., Part II. and the Staff Manual respectively. Title pages will be prepared in manuscript.

WAR DIARY
or
INTELLIGENCE SUMMARY.
(Erase heading not required.)

Army Form C. 2118.

Place	Date	Hour	Summary of Events and Information	Remarks and references to Appendices
	28.		Battalion occupied in improving billets in FRETIN. Educational classes started. Major. J. CRUICKSHANK struck off strength on posting to 36th N.F. 24-10-18. 6. O.R's joined. 1. O.R. evacuated sick.	
	29.		Battalion commenced training in FRETIN Area. 2/Lt. J.R. McCALLUM rejoined from hospital. " J.W. HILL " " " 13. O.R's joined 2 O'R's evacuated sick.	
	30.		Battalion continued training in FRETIN Area. 1 O.R joined 1 O.R. evacuated sick 2 O.R's transferred to Transportation Troops Depot CALAIS	

D. D. & L., London, E.C.
(A10266) Wt W5300/P713 750,000 2/18 Sch. 52 Forms/C2118/16.

App. I.

SECRET.

Copy No. 10/3

Operation Orders,
by Capt J.R.PHILIP, M.C.,
Commanding.

No.26
SATURDAY
2-11-18.

1. 9th Black Watch will be relieved by 18th Scottish Rifles about mid-day on November 3rd.
   On relief Black Watch will take over area vacated by Scottish Rifles at LES ESCOBELLES.

2. Order of March.
   B, C, M, A, Coys. Transport.
   200 yards interval between Companies.
   Cooker and L.G.Limber with Companies.
   Dress:- Full marching Order. Aprons in the packs.
   Route:- [illegible] - X in [illegible] - [illegible] CROSS ROADS - LES ESCOBELLES.

3. Blankets to be neatly rolled in bundles of ten, labelled and stacked at Q.M.Stores by 1000.
   Officers valises at Q.M.Stores by 1000.
   Mess stores to be carried by companies.

4. Time of moving to be detailed later.

5. All billets and latrines to be left clean and a certificate to this effect to be rendered to the Adjutant before moving off.

[signature]

Issued at 0700

Capt & Adjt.,
9th (S) Battn The Black Watch.

Copies to
1/5 Coys.
6 C.O.
7 Q.M.
8 T.O.
9 R.S.M.
10. File.

app II

SECRET 9th (S) Battn The Black Watch. Copy No. 9

Operation Orders.
by Capt J.R.PHILIP, M.C.,
Commanding.

No. 27
SUNDAY
10-11-18.

Reference TOURNAI 5.

1. Intention. 9th Black Watch will move today to Area LONGUE SAULE [illegible] BOURGAGE.

2. Order of March. H.Q., A.,B.D.C. Coys. transport. 200 yards interval between Coys. Mess and Maltese cart march behind Battn H.Q. Coy. Cookers and Limbers behind Coys.

3. Starting Point. Road junction North of N. in O[illegible]H . move of at 0930

4. Dress. Full marching order less aprons.

5. Kits. C,D. Coys. and H.Qrs officers kits and blankets at Q.M.Stores by 0800. A & B Coys. officers kits and blankets at A Coy. H.Q. by 0800.

6. Advance Party. 2/Lt.PATTULLO and 1 N.C.O.for H.Qrs. 1 officer per Coy. and 1 N.C.O. per platoon will rendezvous at A Coy. H.Qrs at 0830 to proceed to new area as billeting party.

7. Companies will report disposition and location of new H.Qrs on arrival.

[illegible signature] Hamilton

Capt & Adjt.,
9th (S) Battn The Black Watch.

Issued at. 0715
Copies to
1/4 Coys.
5 Q.M.
6 2/Lt.Pattullo.
7 File.
8 R.S.M.
9 C.O.,

App. III.

SECRET. **9th (S) Battn The Black Watch.** **Copy No. 5**

OPERATION ORDER No.88 FRIDAY 15-11-18.

Referecne sheets 37 and 44.

1. INTENTION:- The 9th Black Watch will move to [illegible] area today.

2. ORDER OF MARCH:- HA. Qrs, B,C,D,A, Coys, transport. 200 yards
   between Companies.
   Mess Cart behind H.Q..
   Coy.Limbers and Cookers behind Coys.
   Maltese Cart behind Battn.

3. DRESS:- Full marching Order less aprons.

4. STARTING POINT:- U.19.c.50.80. at 0945

5. ROUTE:- [illegible]- Forked Road U.13.c.10.50.- [illegible].

6. KITS:- Officers valises,mens blankets and band's packs to be at Q.M.Stores by 0730.

7. ADVANCE PARTY:- 1 off. and 1 N.C.O. for H.Q., 1 off. ~~and 1 N.C.O.~~ per Coy. and 1 N.C.O. per platoon. will rendezvous at Bn H.Q. at 0730 and proceed under 2/Lt.MAIN to new area as billeting party.

8. Companies will report arrival and location of new H.Q.

9. ACKNOWLEDGE.

A.K. Hamilton

Capt & Adjt.,
9th (S) Battn The Black Watch.

Issued at.
Copies to
1/4 Coys.
5 H.Q.
6 2/Lt.MAIN.
7 Q.M.
8 T.O.
9 R.S.M.
10. File.

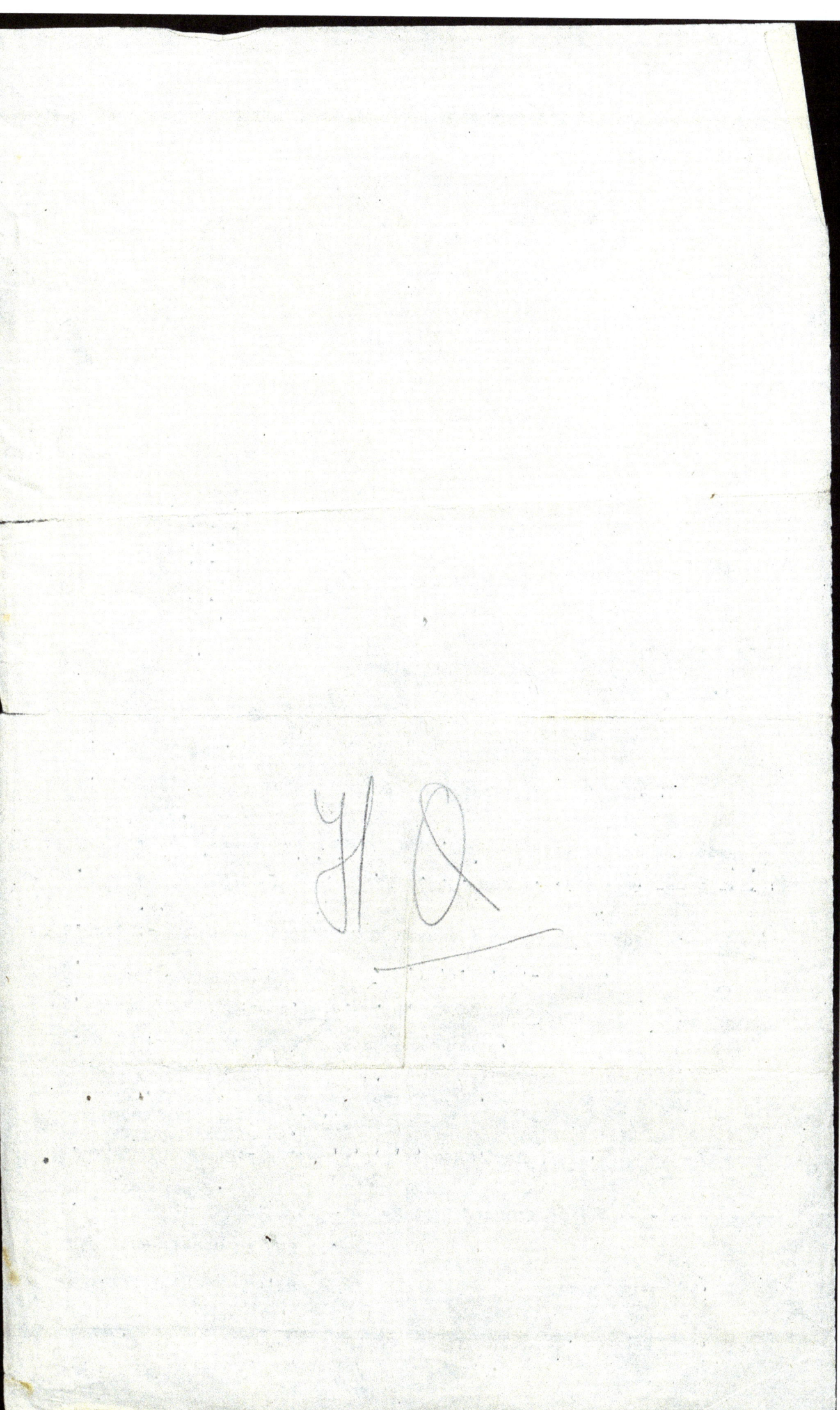

App. IV

SECRET — 9th Bn. the Black Watch Order No. [illegible] Copy No. [illegible]

Reference Sheets 44 & 44A N.E. [illegible] 18

1. Intention :— The 9th Black Watch will move to AVELIN [illegible]

2. Order of March :— Hqrs. D. A. C. B. Transport. 200^x between Coys.
Mess Cart behind Hqrs.
Coy Cookers [illegible] behind Coys.
Maltese Cart behind [illegible].

3. Dress :— Full marching order. [illegible] on packs.

4. Move off from A 4 c. 80. 20. at 0850

5. Route :— GENECH — TEMPLEUVE — ENNEVELIN.

6. Officers' Valises to be stacked outside Coy Hqrs by 0730.
Men's Blankets and [illegible] packs to be stacked outside
Q.M. Stores by 0730.

7. Advance Party :— 1 offr. per Coy and Hqrs and 1 N.C.O. [illegible]
platoon and Bn Hqrs will rendezvous at D. Coy Hqrs at
0730 and proceed under 2/Lt. Pattullo to new Area.

8. Coys will report arrival in new billets

9. ACKNOWLEDGE.

[illegible signature]

Capt & Adjt
9th Bn the Black Watch.

Copies to
1/4 Coys
5 Hqrs ✓
6 2/Lt. Pattullo.
7 Q.M.
8 T.O
[illegible]

App. V

SECRET. 9th (S) Battn The Black Watch Copy No. 10

OPERATION ORDER No.30. TUESDAY, 26-11-18.

Ref.TOURNAI 5.

1. The 9th Black Watch will move to FRETIN tomorrow 27-11-18.

2. Order of March:- H.Q.
B Coy.
C "
D "
A "
Transport.

3. Route:- AVELIN - FRETIN.

4. Dress:- Full marching order. Aprons in packs. Jerkins to be worn under S.D.jackets.

5. Parade:- Parade in Close Column on the parade ground at 1015.

6. Advance Party:- 1 off. per coy. and Battn H.Q.,4 N.C.Os per Coy. and 2 for Battn H.Q. parade at Battn H.Q. at 0900 to proceed under 2/Lt.PATULLO to billet.

7. Kits of Officers billeted in CHATEAU to be stacked outside the Chateau by 0830. Kits of all other officers to be stacked at Q.M.Stores by 0830.
Blankets to be rolled in bundles of 10 and stacked at Q.M.Stores by 0830.

8. ACKNOWLEDGE.

J.K. Hamilton

Capt & Adjt.,
9th (S) Battn The Black Watch.

Issued at
Copies to:-
1/4 Coys.
5 C.O.
6 Q.M.
7.T.O.
8.2/Lt.Patullo.
9.R.S.M.
10.H.Q.
11.File.

In addition to party detailed in para 6, each coy will send 2 men per platoon.

J.K.H.

Army Form C. 2118.

Instructions regarding War Diaries and Intelligence Summaries are contained in F. S. Regs., Part II. and the Staff Manual respectively. Title pages will be prepared in manuscript.

WAR DIARY
or
~~INTELLIGENCE SUMMARY.~~

(Erase heading not required.)

Place	Date	Hour	Summary of Events and Information	Remarks and references to Appendices
			9th (S). Bn The Black Watch War Diary for December 1918. Volume XI	

Alex. J. Stewart Lieut.-Colonel,
Commanding 9th (S) Bn The Black Watch.

Instructions regarding War Diaries and Intelligence Summaries are contained in F. S. Regs., Part II. and the Staff Manual respectively. Title pages will be prepared in manuscript.

WAR DIARY
or
~~INTELLIGENCE~~ SUMMARY.

(Erase heading not required.)

Army Form C. 2118.

Place	Date	Hour	Summary of Events and Information	Remarks and references to Appendices
	1.		Battalion still training in FRETIN	
			2/Lt. A.W. MACDONALD gazetted as LIEUTENANT on Nov. 26th 1918.	
			2 men joined	
			4 " evacuated sick.	
	2.		Battalion training in FRETIN Area	
			Major J R PHILIP, M.C. to wear badge of Rank (D.R.O. 769 1.12.18)	
			1 man joined	
			3 men evacuated sick	
	3.		From this date till note made to the contrary the Battalion is training in FRETIN Area	
			Result of Inter-Coy. Cross-Country Run was B. D. A & C. Coys	
			28 men joined.	
			1 man evacuated sick	
			1 " to 47th Trench Mortar Battery	
			4 " to PERTH for exchange.	
	4.		3 men joined.	

A5834 Wt. W4973/M687 750,000 8/16 D. D. & L. Ltd. Forms/C.2118/13

Instructions regarding War Diaries and Intelligence Summaries are contained in F. S. Regs., Part II. and the Staff Manual respectively. Title pages will be prepared in manuscript.

WAR DIARY
or
INTELLIGENCE SUMMARY.

(*Erase heading not required.*)

Army Form C. 2118.

Place	Date	Hour	Summary of Events and Information	Remarks and references to Appendices
	5		2 men joined	
	6.		No change	
	7.		7 men joined 3 " evacuated sick.	
	8.		1 man joined 2 " evacuated sick.	
	9.		6 men evacuated sick.	
	10		No change	
	11		14 Coalminers left for demobilization	
	12.		25 Coalminers left for demobilization	
	13.		First meeting of Battalion Debating Society. 146 men joined. 3 " evacuated sick	

A5834 Wt. W4973/M687 750,000 8/16 D. D. & L. Ltd. Forms/C.2118/13

Instructions regarding War Diaries and Intelligence Summaries are contained in F. S. Regs., Part II. and the Staff Manual respectively. Title pages will be prepared in manuscript.

WAR DIARY

~~or~~

~~INTELLIGENCE SUMMARY.~~

(Erase heading not required.)

Army Form C. 2118.

Place	Date	Hour	Summary of Events and Information	Remarks and references to Appendices
	14		1 man joined 1 " evacuated sick	
	15.		1 man joined 1 " evacuated sick.	
	16		2 men joined 4 " evacuated sick.	
	17.		21 Coalminers left for demobilization 1 man evacuated sick. 2/Lt. M. LAMBROUGHTON died of Influenza on 16.11.18	
	18.		1 man struck off strength on being transferred to 4/5th Black Watch.	
	19.		1 man struck off strength	
	21		1 man struck off strength.	

A5834 Wt. W4973/M687 750,000 8/16 D. D. & L. Ltd. Forms/C.2118/13

Instructions regarding War Diaries and Intelligence Summaries are contained in F. S. Regs., Part II. and the Staff Manual respectively. Title pages will be prepared in manuscript.

WAR DIARY
~~or~~
~~INTELLIGENCE SUMMARY.~~

(Erase heading not required.)

Army Form C. 2118.

Place	Date	Hour	Summary of Events and Information	Remarks and references to Appendices
	22.		2/Lt. W. D. WATSON to U.K. for demobilization (Pivotal)	
			1 man to U.K. for demobilization (Pivotal)	
			2 " " " " " (miners).	
			1 " " " " tour of duty.	
			2 men taken on strength.	
	23.		2 men evacuated sick.	
	24		1 man to U.K. for demobilization (long service)	
			1 " evacuated sick	
			1 " taken on strength.	
	25.		2 men evacuated sick.	
			Christmas Day. Whole Holiday. Church Services held at 1100.	
	26.		9 men evacuated sick.	
	27.		2 men to U.K. for demobilization (long service).	

A5834 Wt. W4973/M687 750,000 8/16 D. D. & L. Ltd. Forms/C.2118/13

Instructions regarding War Diaries and Intelligence Summaries are contained in F. S. Regs., Part II. and the Staff Manual respectively. Title pages will be prepared in manuscript.

WAR DIARY
or
~~INTELLIGENCE SUMMARY.~~

(Erase heading not required.)

Army Form C. 2118.

Place	Date	Hour	Summary of Events and Information	Remarks and references to Appendices
	28.		2/Lt. A.M. WILKIE to U.K. for demobilization (Pivotal).	
			6 men to U.K. for demobilization (miners).	
			1 " " " " " (pivotal).	
			2 " " " " " (long service).	
			1 man taken on strength.	
	31.		1 man taken on strength.	

A5834 Wt. W4973/M687 750,000 8/16 D. D. & L. Ltd. Forms/C.2118/13

Instructions regarding War Diaries and Intelligence Summaries are contained in F. S. Regs., Part II. and the Staff Manual respectively. Title pages will be prepared in manuscript.

WAR DIARY
or
INTELLIGENCE SUMMARY.
(Erase heading not required.)

Army Form C. 2118.

FTP

VR 43

Place	Date	Hour	Summary of Events and Information	Remarks and references to Appendices

9th (S). Btn the Black Watch

War Diary

for

January 1919.

Volume XII

B 40

3-2-19.

Alr. J Stewart Lt
Lieut.-Colonel,
Commanding. 9th (S) Btn The Black Watch.

A5834 Wt. W4973/M687 750,000 8/16 D. D. & L. Ltd. Forms/C.2118/13

Instructions regarding War Diaries and Intelligence Summaries are contained in F. S. Regs., Part II. and the Staff Manual respectively. Title pages will be prepared in manuscript.

WAR DIARY

or

~~INTELLIGENCE SUMMARY.~~

(Erase heading not required.)

Army Form C. 2118.

Place	Date	Hour	Summary of Events and Information	Remarks and references to Appendices
	3.		6 men proceeded to U.K for demobn. 3 " " " " " 28 days' leave under G.R.O. 5951. 3 " evacuated sick 1 " taken on strength	
	4.		5 men taken on strength	
	6.		2 men taken on strength 1 man evac. sick 1 " struck off strength	
	7.		1 man struck off strength	
	8.		3 men taken on strength	
	9		2 men evac. sick. Battalion Boxing Competition was held to choose competitors for Divl. Tournament.	
	10.		2 men evac. sick. 1 " struck off strength.	

D. D. & L., London, E.C.
(A10266) Wt W5300/P713 750,000 2/18 Sch. 52 Forms/C2118/16.

Army Form C. 2118.

WAR DIARY
or
INTELLIGENCE SUMMARY.
(Erase heading not required.)

Instructions regarding War Diaries and Intelligence Summaries are contained in F. S. Regs., Part II. and the Staff Manual respectively. Title pages will be prepared in manuscript.

Place	Date	Hour	Summary of Events and Information	Remarks and references to Appendices
	11		31 men to U.K. for demobn. 4 " " " " 28 days leave under G.R.O. 5951 and struck off strength. 2/Lts E.R.C. WALKER and A.J. CAMERON to U.K. for demobn.	
	12.		3 men taken on strength.	
	13.		3 men to U.K for demobn.	
	14		4 men taken on strength.	
	15.		1 man evac sick.	
	16.		Final Battalion Boxing Competition was held and winners chosen to represent Battalion in Divisional Competition	
	17.		3 men evac sick.	
	18.		25 men to U.K. for demobn. Lieut. J.R. FAIRLEY to U.K. for demobn.	
	19.		1 man taken on strength.	

D. D. & L., London, E.C.
(A10266) Wt W5300/P715 750,000 2/18 Sch. 52 Forms/C2118/16.

Instructions regarding War Diaries and Intelligence Summaries are contained in F. S. Regs., Part II. and the Staff Manual respectively. Title pages will be prepared in manuscript.

WAR DIARY
or
INTELLIGENCE SUMMARY.
(*Erase heading not required.*)

Army Form C. 2118.

Place	Date	Hour	Summary of Events and Information	Remarks and references to Appendices
	20.		1 man evac. sick. Lieut F. L. McGRADY evac sick 28/11/18.	
	21		12 men to U.K. for demobn. 1 man evac. sick.	
	22		3 men to U.K. for demobn. 3 " demobilized while in U.K.	
	23.		1 man off strength.	
	25.		62 men to U.K. for demobn 2/Lt. K. W. B. SANDERSON to U.K. for demobn.	
	27.		31 men to U.K. for demobn. 2 men demobilized while in U.K. 1 " taken on strength.	
	28.		26 men to U.K. for demobn. 2/Lt. J. WISHART to U.K. for demobn.	

A5834 Wt. W4973/M687 750,000 8/16 D. D. & L. Ltd. Forms/C.2118/13

Army Form C. 2118.

Instructions regarding War Diaries and Intelligence Summaries are contained in F. S. Regs., Part II. and the Staff Manual respectively. Title pages will be prepared in manuscript.

WAR DIARY
or
~~INTELLIGENCE SUMMARY.~~
(Erase heading not required.)

Place	Date	Hour	Summary of Events and Information	Remarks and references to Appendices
	30		3 men demobilized while in U.K. 1 man taken on strength.	
	31.		Divisional Boxing Competition commenced at PONT-A-MARCQ.	

A5834 Wt. W4973/M687 750,000 8/16 D. D. & L. Ltd. Forms/C.2118/13

9th Black Watch No. A.W. 1935

Instructions regarding War Diaries and Intelligence Summaries are contained in F. S. Regs., Part II. and the Staff Manual respectively. Title pages will be prepared in manuscript.

WAR DIARY
or
INTELLIGENCE SUMMARY.

(Erase heading not required.)

Army Form C. 2118.

VR 44

Place	Date	Hour	Summary of Events and Information	Remarks and references to Appendices
			9th (S) Bn. The Black Watch	
			War Diary	B 41
			No.	
			February 19	
			Vol. XIII	
2.3.17			R.L.Kilgour Capt. for Commanding	

D. D. & L., London, E.C.
(A10266) Wt W5300/P713 750,000 2/18 Sch. 52 Forms/C2118/16.

Instructions regarding War Diaries and Intelligence Summaries are contained in F. S. Regs., Part II. and the Staff Manual respectively. Title pages will be prepared in manuscript.

WAR DIARY

or

INTELLIGENCE SUMMARY.

(Erase heading not required.)

Army Form C. 2118.

Place	Date	Hour	Summary of Events and Information	Remarks and references to Appendices
	1.		Finals of Divisional Boxing Competition were held at PONT A MARCQ 1 man taken on strength Lieut J. Callan demobilized while on leave	
	2.		3 men evac. sick The Kings Colours were presented to the Battalion of 47 Inf. Bde by H.R.H. the Prince of Wales at PONT A MARCQ	
	3.		3 men to U.K. for demobilization	
	4		1 man taken on strength	
	5		1 Man evacuated sick	
	6		1 man evacuated sick 2 Lt [illegible] Burt and 53 O.R. to U.K. for demobilization	

D. D. & L., London, E.C.
(A10266) Wt W5300/P713 750,000 2/18 Sch. 52 Forms/C2118/16.

Instructions regarding War Diaries and Intelligence Summaries are contained in F. S. Regs., Part II. and the Staff Manual respectively. Title pages will be prepared in manuscript.

WAR DIARY
or
INTELLIGENCE SUMMARY.
(Erase heading not required.)

Army Form C. 2118.

Place	Date	Hour	Summary of Events and Information	Remarks and references to Appendices
	7		6 men to U.K. for demob. 1 man evacuated sick	
	8		23 men to U.K. for demobilization	
	9		1 man [illegible] 9 men to U.K. for demobilization	
	10		Major [illegible] struck off strength from 13-1-19 pending demob. 2 men [illegible] [illegible]	
	12		1 man evac. sick	
	13		39 OR to U.K. for demob. 1 man taken on strength	
	14		15 OR to U.K. for demob. Capt. [illegible] and Capt. [illegible] M.C. to U.K. [illegible] demob. struck off strength	

D. D. & L., London, E.C.
(A10266) Wt W5300/P713 750,000 2/18 Sch. 52 Forms/C2118/16.

Instructions regarding War Diaries and Intelligence Summaries are contained in F. S. Regs., Part II. and the Staff Manual respectively. Title pages will be prepared in manuscript.

WAR DIARY
or
INTELLIGENCE SUMMARY.
(*Erase heading not required.*)

Army Form C. 2118.

Place	Date	Hour	Summary of Events and Information	Remarks and references to Appendices
	15		12 men to U.K. for demobilization 1 man taken on strength Lieut. D. R. Reid assumed duties of [illegible]	
	16		1 man demobilized while on leave 8 men to U.K. for demob.	
	17		1 man taken on strength	
	18		1 man evacuated sick	
	19		6 men to U.K. for demob. 1 man taken on strength 1 man evacuated sick	
	20		16 men to U.K. for demob. Capt. [illegible] Proudfoot M.C. to U.K. for demobilization 1 man taken on strength	

D. D. & L., London, E.C.
(A10266) Wt W5300/P713 750,000 2/18 Sch. 52 Forms/C2118/16.

Instructions regarding War Diaries and Intelligence Summaries are contained in F. S. Regs., Part II. and the Staff Manual respectively. Title pages will be prepared in manuscript.

WAR DIARY
or
INTELLIGENCE SUMMARY.
(Erase heading not required.)

Army Form C. 2118.

Place	Date	Hour	Summary of Events and Information	Remarks and references to Appendices
	22		12 men to U.K. for [illegible] 2 men evacuated sick 2 men taken on strength	
	23		6 men struck off strength [illegible] Concentration Camps	
	24		8 men to U.K. for [illegible]	
	25		[illegible]	
	26		[illegible] Capt R [illegible] assumed [illegible]	
	27		9 men to U.K. for [illegible]	
	28		23 men to U.K. for [illegible] 6 men evacuated sick 1 man taken on strength	

D. D. & L., London, E.C.
(A10266) Wt W5300/P713 750,000 2/18 Sch. 52 Forms/C2118/16.

B.W. 1213

Army Form C. 2118.

Instructions regarding War Diaries and Intelligence Summaries are contained in F. S. Regs., Part II. and the Staff Manual respectively. Title pages will be prepared in manuscript.

WAR DIARY
or
~~INTELLIGENCE SUMMARY.~~
(Erase heading not required.)

VB 45

Place	Date	Hour	Summary of Events and Information	Remarks and references to Appendices
			9th (S) Bn. The Black Watch (R.H.)	
			War Diary	
			for	
			March 1919	
			Volume XIV.	B 42
	2.4.19		R.K. Kilgour Capt. for Lieut. Colonel Commanding 9th (S) Battn. The Black Watch	

D. D. & L., London, E.C.
(A10266) Wt W5300/P713 750,000 2/18 Sch. 52 Forms/C2118/16.

Instructions regarding War Diaries and Intelligence Summaries are contained in F. S. Regs., Part II. and the Staff Manual respectively. Title pages will be prepared in manuscript.

WAR DIARY

or

~~INTELLIGENCE~~ SUMMARY.

(*Erase heading not required.*)

Army Form C. 2118.

Place	Date	Hour	Summary of Events and Information	Remarks and references to Appendices
Fretin	1.		One man proceeded to U.K. on 3 months leave under A.O. IV of 10.12.18	
	2.		One Officer proceeded on leave.	
	4.		One man evacuated sick.	
	6.		Two men proceeded to U.K. on leave.	
			Two Officers proceeded to U.K. on leave.	
			One man evacuated sick.	
	8		One man proceeded to U.K. on 3 months leave under A.O. IV of 10.12.18	
			One man to U.K. for demobilization.	
			Two men taken on strength.	
			One officer granted leave in U.K. on completion of draft conducting duty.	
	10.		Five Officers and One hundred & eighty five other ranks proceeded to the 1/6 Black Watch in the Army of Occupation.	
	11.		Three Officers and fifty four other ranks proceeded to join the 1/6th Black Watch in the Army of Occupation.	
			One Officer proceeded on two months leave (Regulars)	
			One man evacuated sick.	

D. D. & L., London, E.C.
(A10266) Wt W5300/P713 750,000 2/18 Sch. 52 Forms/C2118/16.

Army Form C. 2118.

WAR DIARY
or
~~INTELLIGENCE~~ SUMMARY.
(Erase heading not required.)

Instructions regarding War Diaries and Intelligence Summaries are contained in F. S. Regs., Part II. and the Staff Manual respectively. Title pages will be prepared in manuscript.

Place	Date	Hour	Summary of Events and Information	Remarks and references to Appendices
Fretin	12.		One man evacuated sick	
	13.		Two men to U.K. on 3 Months leave under A.O. IV. of 10-12-18	
			3 Officers proceeded on 2 Months leave to U.K. (Regulars.)	
	14.		One Officer proceeded to join the 8th Black Watch	
	15.		Two men to Etaples, as Clerks.	
	16.		Five men to U.K. for 3 Months leave under A.O. IV of 10-12-18.	
			Five men to U.K. for 2 Months leave under A.O. IV of 10-12-18.	
	17.		Two Officers to U.K. for demobilisation	
	19.		One man to Etaples as a Clerk	
			R.A.O.C. Staff/Sgt. proceeded to D.A.D.O.S. 16th Division	
			L/Cpl reduced to Ranks & forfeits one days pay by C.O.	
	25.		Three men to U.K. on 3 Months leave under A.O. IV of 10-12-18.	
			Two men to U.K. on 2 Months leave under A.O. IV of 10-12-18.	
			One Officer to U.K. for demobilization	
			One man to U.K. on special leave	
	26.		Battn ~~stopped~~ moved from Fretin to Pont A Marcq	

D. D. & L., London, E.C.
(A10266) Wt W5300/P713 750,000 2/18 Sch. 52 Forms/C2118/16.

Instructions regarding War Diaries and Intelligence Summaries are contained in F. S. Regs., Part II. and the Staff Manual respectively. Title pages will be prepared in manuscript.

WAR DIARY
or
~~INTELLIGENCE SUMMARY.~~
(Erase heading not required.)

Army Form C. 2118.

Place	Date	Hour	Summary of Events and Information	Remarks and references to Appendices
	30		Four Officers to U.K. for demobilization Seven men to U.K. on 3. months leave under A.O. IV of 10.12.18. One man to U.K. on 2. months leave under A.O. IV of 10.12.18	

A5834 Wt. W4973/M687 750,000 8/16 D. D. & L. Ltd. Forms/C.2118/13

Instructions regarding War Diaries and Intelligence Summaries are contained in F. S. Regs., Part II. and the Staff Manual respectively. Title pages will be prepared in manuscript.

WAR DIARY
or
~~INTELLIGENCE SUMMARY.~~

(Erase heading not required.)

Army Form C. 2118.

Place	Date	Hour	Summary of Events and Information	Remarks and references to Appendices
			9th (S.) Battn. The Black Watch (R. H.)	
			War Diary	
			for	
			April 1919	
			Volume XV	

R Kilgour capt. Lieut.-Colonel
Commanding 9th (S) Bn. The Black Watch

2.5.19

B43

D. D. & L., London, E.C.
(A10266) Wt W5300/P713 750,000 2/18 Sch. 52 Forms/C2118/16.

Instructions regarding War Diaries and Intelligence Summaries are contained in F. S. Regs., Part II. and the Staff Manual respectively. Title pages will be prepared in manuscript.

WAR DIARY
or
INTELLIGENCE SUMMARY.
(Erase heading not required.)

Army Form C. 2118.

Place	Date	Hour	Summary of Events and Information	Remarks and references to Appendices
Pont A. Mancq	2.		One man proceeded to U.K. on leave.	
			One man taken on strength.	
			Two men admitted to Hospital.	
			Attached A.G.S. instructor to U.K. on leave.	
	6.		One man proceeded to U.K. on leave.	
			One man to U.K. on 3 months leave under A.O. IV. 10.12.18.	
			One man to U.K. on 2 months leave under. A.O. IV of 10.12.18.	
			One officer to U.K. for demobilization.	
			One man evacuated sick.	
	10.		Two men proceeded to U.K. on 14 days leave.	
			Padre proceeded to army of Occupation.	
	13.		One man to U.K. for 14 days leave.	
			One officer to U.K. for 14 days leave.	
	17.		Two men to U.K. on 14 days leave.	
	21.		One man to U.K. on 14 days leave.	
			One man struck off strength on proceeding to Home Records.	

D. D. & L., London, E.C.
(A10266) Wt W5300/P713 750,000 2/18 Sch. 52 Forms/C2118/16.

Army Form C. 2118.

WAR DIARY
or
INTELLIGENCE SUMMARY.

(Erase heading not required.)

Instructions regarding War Diaries and Intelligence Summaries are contained in F. S. Regs., Part II. and the Staff Manual respectively. Title pages will be prepared in manuscript.

Place	Date	Hour	Summary of Events and Information	Remarks and references to Appendices
Pont A Marcq	22.		One man to U.K. on 14-days leave	
			Twenty one men transferred to 1/6th Black Watch in Army of Occupation, off strength	
	25.		One man to U.K. on 14 days leave.	
			One man demobilized.	
	28.		One man to U.K. on 28-days special agricultural leave.	
			One man taken on strength.	

D. D. & L., London, E.C.
(A10266) Wt W5300/P713 750,000 2/18 Sch. 52 Forms/C2118/16.

www.ingramcontent.com/pod-product-compliance
Lightning Source LLC
Chambersburg PA
CBHW081447160426
43193CB00013B/2400

* 9 7 8 1 4 7 4 5 0 9 9 7 8 *